MOTHERS & SONS

MOTHERS & SONS

Madeleine L'Engle

Photography by
Maria Rooney

HAROLD SHAW PUBLISHERS

ISBN 0-87788-567-2

Cover and interior design by David LaPlaca

Library of Congress Cataloging-in-Publication Data

L'Engle, Madeleine.
     Mothers and sons / text by Madeleine L'Engle ; photography by Maria Rooney.
        p. cm.
     ISBN 0-87788-567-2 (cloth)
     1. Mothers and sons—Miscellanea. 2. Mothers and sons—Pictorial works. I. Rooney, Maria.
     II. Title.
     HQ755.85.L452 1999
     306.874'3—dc21   98-55387
                                               CIP

03 02 01 00 99

10 9 8 7 6 5 4 3 2 1

CONTENTS

PREFACE — Madeleine L'Engle

It is a special joy to work on a book with my photographer daughter. When we did *Mothers and Daughters*, Maria took the pictures to go with my text. With *Mothers and Sons* we have used the opposite technique. Maria gave me a sheaf of pictures from which I wrote the text.

When I finished, I showed a friend the texts with the pictures. She said about one, "But she doesn't play tennis."

I replied, "I have no way of knowing whether she does or not. From the picture, she is to me a woman who would enjoy playing tennis with her son, and she's just as good as he is, or maybe better."

My friend turned to another picture with its text. "She looks like a friend of mine who was divorced a year ago, and basically she doesn't like men."

"I have no way of knowing that," I said. "All I can do is look at the pictures and see what they have to tell me. That may be quite different from the actual facts, but it's what the pictures say to me. The people in the bookstore who pick up the book aren't going to have personal knowledge of these mothers and sons either. They, too, will be seeing strangers. Like me, they will be making stories from what they see in the pictures. They are wonderful pictures, full of love, and they trigger the imagination. I am writing from what I see in the pictures."

I could not write what I write if my daughter didn't have the pictures for me. I think it's an exciting way to work, and I have loved doing it.

INTRODUCTION — Maria Rooney

I never wanted to be a mother. For many years I was afraid that if I became a mother I would automatically die after seven years of parenthood. This is because my father died when I was six years old, and then my mother died when I was seven. I thought it was a curse. I was quickly adopted by Madeleine and Hugh, so they became my legal parents—my new mother and father. But still, I never really believed in the longevity of parents.

When I became old enough to think of having children of my own, I didn't. I told myself that I didn't really like children anyway. I more or less steered clear of babies.

At the age of thirty I realized that I was probably destined never to have children, and I was okay with that. I was divorced, working at my photography, and having a wonderful time. Then, just when I least expected it, I met my husband, John. It was almost love at first sight, and we got married and had two baby boys seventeen months apart.

Now we are a lively family with one teenager and one soon to be. The nerves get frazzled with the usual crises and dramas and victories; but we all get through it together. Boys make for a rather noisy house, but as Mother says, as long as it is happy noise it is okay. I get impatient with incessant soccer and dirty, dirty clothes. Yet when I wish the family phone would leave my son's ear occasionally, I suddenly remember that the boys will be on their own in just a few years. And I wouldn't trade the boisterous, boy-filled house for anything!

MANY
MILESTONES

He's always hungry, my beautiful boy. Now he's chewing my shoulder. Dribbling. My blouse will dry in the sun. So will the little outfit my grandmother gave him. She's a great-grandmother now. I wonder if that will happen to me, if time will go on and on, and my boy will grow and marry and have babies and they'll grow and marry—

It's so far off I can't think about it right now. Right now it's just the warm sun and the summer afternoon and my little boy who is hungry for love. And for me.

There he is, every bit of him, my boy, my baby. He's quiet, now, fed and content. I can forget being waked up in the night with him screaming with hunger or colic. I'm underslept, like most moms. That's how it goes. But it's so good this afternoon, sitting here in the sun. And he's happy, and I'm happy.

I wonder what he'll be like when he grows up?

I'm putting my son to bed. He's still little enough for me to do that, but he won't be for long. Meanwhile I enjoy pulling his T-shirt over his head. Easing off his trousers. Kissing his ears to make him laugh. Why do we lose this early spontaneity? What does the world do to us that we pull away from each other?

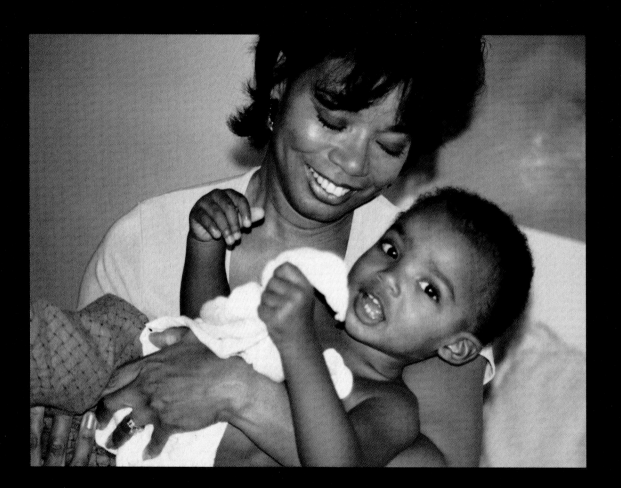

I hold my son, almost the way I did when he was a baby. He still leans against me, as though I am part of his body, and exist only for that reason. To be, for him. Later he will have to be, for himself. But not quite yet.

He's holding his bottle, and I tease him by pulling it away. It's different, the bottle from the breast. What is the same is the love. One way or the other, I nourish him. I help him grow. I will try to teach him to tell the truth, never to lie. I will try to teach him to be honorable and brave.

Oh, my son, what a responsibility you are!

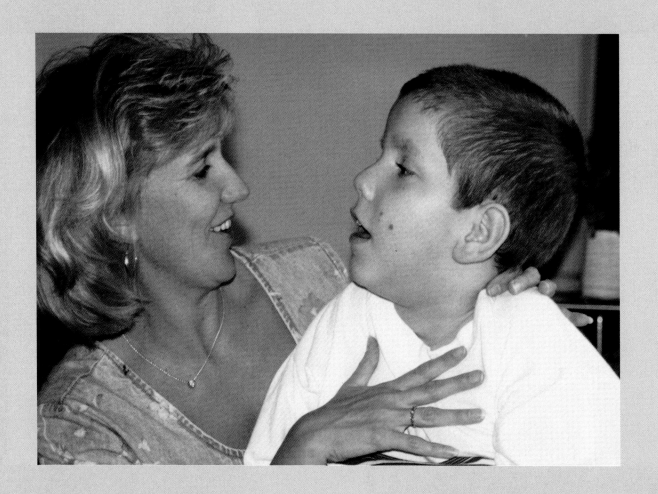

When I fell off my bike, I hurt my back, and I have to do special exercises to make it strong again. It's much better than it was at first, but I still have a way to go to catch up with the other kids. I'll get there. The doctor agrees. She says I'm stubborn and I won't quit, and that's the best way to be. I like her.

I had to have a shot today. It hurt. I mean, it really hurt. I didn't scream. I just gave a sort of grunt. I told the nurse I didn't need a pain pill. I was okay. My mom says she's proud of me.

I like it when people say, "Oh, but you can't be their mother! You must be their sister! You look so young."

But I don't think the kids like it. It doesn't make me any less their mother, but they think it does. Of course I'm their mother, but that's not all I am. I am myself, too. One day they'll be gone, raising their own families, doing their own thing. Can't I be both mother and me?

We're proud of each other, my son and I. I'm in law school, a little older than some of the students, but there are things I need to know. In a few years he'll be in law school, too, and he'll ask me to help him with his homework, the way he used to with arithmetic.

My little one is bright as a button. He's in a school for bright kids, but it hasn't gone to his head. His father and I have taught him that everybody is special, and he's special, too, and maybe extra special to me, but I don't tell him that.

My son is still young enough to hug and be hugged. His face still feels soft. There's no roughness on his cheeks. I love to hug and be hugged. My husband didn't hug his mother for years, but now that she's growing old he hugs her again the way he did when he was a little boy.

Hugs are good.

Maybe it's the beard. I look in the mirror and see myself with my son and he looks old enough to be—my brother, at least. Or maybe I don't realize how old I really am. But I look in the mirror and I like what I see there.

I fell over a step and broke my ankle. I wanted to cry because I felt so stupid, not because my ankle hurt. My kids told me they'd done stupid things, too, like falling out of a tree and breaking an arm, or falling off a bike and skinning both knees. My littlest son fell all the way down a flight of stairs and didn't break anything. How I love them!

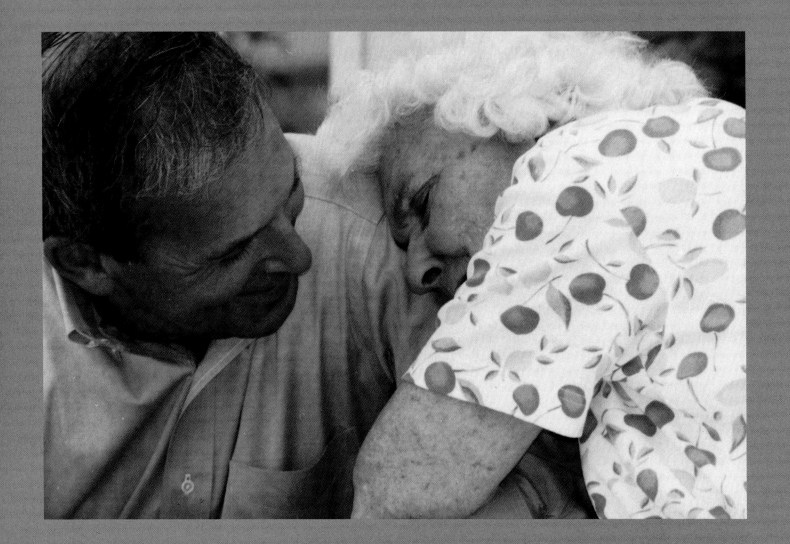

My son holds me the way I held him when I was a young mom. It feels strange, and it feels good. And the pain doesn't hurt so much anymore.

I tell my son he shouldn't work so hard. He smiles, and I know he's going to pay no attention to me. He says, "Hey, Mom, you're the pot talking to the kettle." He laughs at me. His dad laughs, too, and says we're like two peas in a pod. It's true. But work is good. Don't complain.

My son tells me a funny story, and I
laugh. It is wonderful to be amused by
the same things, to laugh together.

THINGS WE
DO TOGETHER

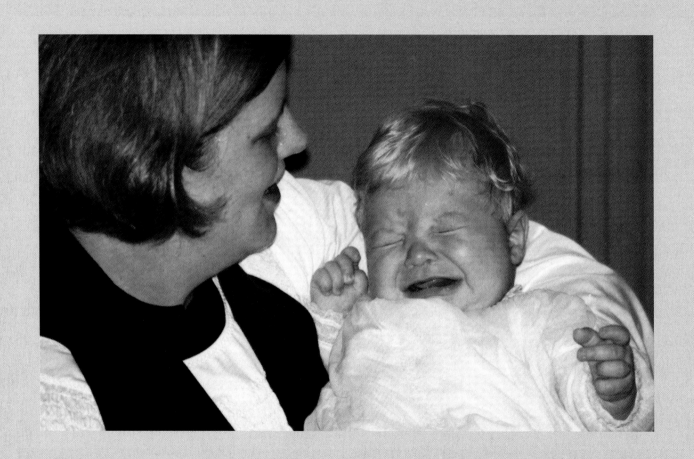

What a howl of rage! How you squint your eyes, fold your hands into fists, yowl your displeasure! What do you want? Your diapers are dry. I just fed you. Is it sleep you are fighting? You are so funny! And if I laugh at you, you just yell louder.

Go to sleep, little one. Go to sleep.

This is your Name Day, the day you are given to God and given to your name. There is something special about this day, when you are given to God forever and gifted with your very own name. You are no less mine, but now you belong to God in a special way.

There he is, my beautiful boy, looking like some special toy in one of the big toy shops. My husband says, "He's not a toy. He's our son. Maybe he'll be president of the United States one day." I don't care about that. He's a good baby. I just want him to be a good man.

Patty cake, patty cake. He's not old enough to say the words or hit my hands with his in the old patty-cake rhythm. He's growing so quickly. He'll get there before I know it.

Patty cake.

If anybody had told me a year ago that I'd enjoy being slobbered over, I wouldn't have believed it. But baby slobber is part of baby kissing, and I wouldn't miss it. I love my little slobberer.

He's beginning to notice so much, my little one. "That's a pear," I say. Or, "That's an apple." Or an orange, or a tennis ball. I kiss his soft little cheek. Babies smell so good!

We look at ourselves in a bright ball that's like a mirror, like the mirror in the funny houses at the fair. Would I recognize us if we really looked like that? Would my own mother know me?

My little boy has long, firm legs. He has strong hands. He has a big smile. He lifts his face to the warm, summer rays. We are perfectly happy, mother and son.

My younger son is still at the touchy-feely age. Putting his hand on my head, messing with my hair. Touching. Hugging. My older son has pulled back a little, standing back, but touching finger to finger. He looks at me and grins, and I put my hand on his knee. It is a quiet moment in a busy day, and I am grateful for it.

Here I am with all three sons, a mother's treasure. One still has snaggle teeth, but all three are growing up. Soon they'll all be taller than I am. But I'll never forget their warm, clean, baby bodies, or their first steps, their first attempts at putting words into sentences. My sons. My wonderful sons.

My middle son. It's not easy to be the middle child. He always feels he's being compared with his brothers. No. I love him for who he is, as I love each one for who he is.

We can still go on adventures together, my son and I. And at night he still wants me to read to him, and then to sing the songs I've sung to him all his life. Sometimes I find myself humming these songs as I clean my house, or stand on the corner waiting for the bus. These songs will always mean my son for me.

His hair is still wet from swimming. He looks down, not meeting the mother-intimacy in my eyes. He is growing up, moving away, a little embarrassed at becoming his own self. But that time has come.

How quickly they grow up! One in college, one in grad school. They both think they know a great deal more than I do in all subjects. Maybe they do. But I'm no dummy. I read at night, when the house is quiet, when my husband is snoring beside me, and I can clip onto the side of the book my little reading light. I can't let them get too far ahead of me!

They still kiss me good night. And good morning. And sometimes in between. There may come a time when kissing will embarrass them. When kissing is only for girls. And that is right and proper. But I'm glad we're still at a time when they kiss me.

MOM & ME

That's me, a long time ago, so long I don't remember. Her hair's the same, soft and fair and pretty. I'm the one that's changed. When she used to throw me up in the air and then catch me, we'd both laugh and laugh, and I don't even know what we were laughing about, except fun, and that my mommy loved me and I loved my mommy.

We still love each other, but I've changed, and it's different.

We have a secret, my mom and I. It's my dad's birthday and I've painted him a picture, and my mom is going to mat it so it will look almost like it's framed. Then I'll wrap it in birthday paper. My dad is funny. One year he wrapped all his Christmas packages in newspaper, and tied them with bright red ribbons. He's good at finding out secrets, but we won't let him in on this one.

My mom says the picture I painted is terrific. She let me use her paints, and I was careful not to squeeze the tubes out of shape. I get into trouble with my mom at least once a day, so it's good to hear her telling me I've done something terrific. Terrific. That's her pet word, and when she kisses me good night she tells me that I'm terrible and terrific, but mostly terrific. Yay.

I'm never sure what she's thinking. Her hair's so pretty, and she keeps it soft and clean. I think she loves me; I know she does. But I don't know who's first in her heart. It was okay when it was my dad, but they've been divorced now and he's married again. Is she looking for another dad for me—and someone for herself? How could she find anybody as nice as my dad? Would anybody else love me as much as my dad does? Did. It's my baby sister he has eyes for now, not me.

My mom picked me out of the orphanage when I was very young, three years old. Still, I was one of the last in my building to be picked. My mom says God had me wait so I'd be there for her.

My mom and I don't look alike. Nobody will ever say, "You have your mother's eyes."

I have my mother's love. That's what's important.

Well, I love her and she loves me. She's a good mom as moms go. Doesn't pry into my inner thoughts and dreams like some moms who are into psychology. I can tell that she wants to ask, sometimes, but she doesn't. That's pretty cool.

On the other hand, I don't know what she's thinking, either.

My mom is old. I mean, she's in her thirties. But we still have a lot of fun together. Sometimes I forget how old she is. Sometimes I have to remind her how old I am: sixteen. Birthdays are no longer the milestones they were when I was five and six. But sixteen is special, because now I get to drive the car. Whoopee!

My mom and I can still play together. We play tennis and she has a whopping backhand—though I still win the set. We go hiking together, and swimming. Every year there's less time. Next winter I won't get home from school till after five—after dark for most of the year. The planet turns. The seasons change. I change, too.

When we go to the beach together, Mom forgets that she's a science researcher and knows all about black holes and quasars, and we just relax and tell each other our dreams. Mom would like to move into the city into a big apartment near the hospital where her lab is, so she could just get on a bus or the subway and go to the theatre. I'd like to move to a cabin in the country where every night I could hear the water of the brook, and the animals who come down to drink.

Now that I'm in college the report cards are different than when I was in high school. The work is harder. I have to pay more attention in class, not sit by the window and dream. But my grades are pretty good, and that pleases my mom. Me, too.

She's a wonder, my mom. She doesn't look her age. She has her hair done every week. She puts on makeup, but not too much. She never tries to be younger than she is—but everybody thinks she is. That's because she's willing to be who she is, and who she is is young in heart.

My mother is what the world calls "old." According to chronological years, she is—well up in her eighties. But her mind is still active. She understands politics better than I do because she has more tolerance for human foibles.

We do well, together, my mother and I.

She tries, but she doesn't understand.

When I remind her that she is too old and wobbly on her feet
to stay in the big house with its steep stairs to the sleeping
floors, she just smiles. "I'm very careful. But if I fall I fall. If God
is good it will kill me. If not, you can put me in any kind of
home you like. . . . *Home,* they call these places." She laughs.

"Mom," I say, "it's only because I love you." I wish she'd go of
her own accord. If she won't . . .

Our mom's birthday.

She's 101.

Now she doesn't yell at us and we don't yell at her. She tells us she's proud of us. Her son the doctor. Her son the merchandiser. We're proud of her, too. Nobody would guess she's seen more than a century, or that she married into our family after being hired as a servant so many years ago. She has lived a full life, enriching the world and her family by her joy in living each day. She tells us stories about our world when it was a different world altogether. She is happy in her place in the world of today.